MEN-AT-ARMS SERIES
EDITOR: PHILIP WARNER

Chasseurs of the Guard

THE CHASSEURS À CHEVAL OF THE GARDE IMPÈRIALE
1799–1815

Text by BRIGADIER PETER YOUNG
DSO, MC, MA, FSA, FRHist.S, FRGS

Colour plates by MICHAEL YOUENS

OSPREY PUBLISHING LIMITED

Published in England by
Osprey Publishing Ltd
P.O. Box 25, 707 Oxford Road, Reading, Berkshire
© Copyright 1971 Osprey Publications Ltd

SBN 85045 056 X

I wish to pay tribute to the magnificent work of
the late Commandant E.-L. Bucquoy, historian
of the uniforms of the First Empire.

PETER YOUNG

Printed in Great Britain by
Jarrold & Sons Ltd, Norwich

Chronology

1799

Aug.	General Bonaparte leaves Egypt to return to France; accompanied by 300 of his Guides.
& 10 Nov.	The coup d'état of the 18th Brumaire.
8 Nov.	The *Garde des Consuls* is organized.
7 Dec.	The Guides are in barracks in Paris.

1800

Jan.	A company of *Chasseurs à cheval* is created.
14 June	Battle of Marengo.
Sept.	The corps becomes a squadron of two companies.

1801

Aug.	The corps is increased to two squadrons.
3 Oct.	Bonaparte orders the formation of the Squadron of Mamelukes of the First Consul.
4 Nov.	The Chasseurs become a regiment.

1802

5 Mar.	Treaty of Amiens.
9 May	Creation of the Legion of Honour.
Oct.	The regiment is increased to four squadrons.

1804

21 Jan.	The Mamelukes are attached to the Chasseurs.
18 May	The *Garde des Consuls* becomes the *Garde Impériale*.
2 Dec.	Napoleon is crowned as Emperor of the French.

1805

20 Oct.	Capitulation of Ulm.
2 Dec.	Battle of Austerlitz.

1806

14 Oct.	Battles of Jena and Auerstadt.

1807

8 Feb.	Battle of Eylau.
14 June	Battle of Friedland.

1809

21 May	Battle of Aspern-Essling.
6 July	Battle of Wagram.

1811

16 Sept.	The Emperor orders Marshal Bessières to prepare the Guard to leave on campaign.

1812

24 June	The Grand Army crosses the Niemen.
7 Sept.	Battle of Borodino.
28–29 Nov.	The passage of the Beresina.

1813

26 Aug.	Battle of Dresden.
16–19 Oct.	Battle of Leipzig.

1814

30 Mar.	Fall of Paris.
6 Apr.	First abdication of Napoleon.
14 May	The regiment becomes the *Chasseurs à cheval de France*.
30 May	Treaty of Paris.
28 July	The Regiment is disbanded.
1 Nov.	Opening of the Congress of Vienna.

1815

1 Mar.	Napoleon lands at Golfe-Juan.
21 Mar.	The *Garde Impériale* re-established.
8 Apr.	The Regiment re-formed.
15 May	The creation of a cavalry regiment of *Jeune Garde* is ordered. It is to be attached to and administered by the regiment.
27 May	The new regiment is officially entitled *2ᵉ Régiment de Chasseurs à cheval de la Jeune Garde*.
16 June	The Battles of Ligny and Quatre-Bras.
18 June	The Battle of Waterloo.
22 June	Second abdication of Napoleon.
3 Aug.	King Louis XVIII decrees the dissolution of the Guard.
16 Oct.	Napoleon arrives at St Helena.
26 Oct.	The Regiment's disbandment is ordered.
2 Dec.	The Chasseurs and the Mamelukes disbanded.

1821

5 May	Death of Napoleon.

1840

15 Dec.	Napoleon's ashes are brought back to the banks of the Seine.

Regimental History

'Cavalry needs audacity and practice; above al it must not be dominated by the spirit of con servatism or avarice.'

NAPOLEO

The Regiment had its origins in the Guides raise by General Bonaparte during his Italian Cam paign of 1796. His esteem for the corps i witnessed by the fact that, as Emperor, he almos invariably wore its green undress uniform. Hi Chasseurs were his nearest guard, providing hi immediate escort wherever he went on campaign But they were no mere show troop as they prove in battle after battle.

The excellent spirit that prevailed in the corp is illustrated by an incident related by Parqui one of its officers.

'At Leipzig on 18 October 1813 a chasseu from my troop, one of those who had bee decorated and received a monetary award, ha his horse killed in the battle. I thought he ha returned to the regimental forward depot t obtain a new mount and this would have mean an absence of eight to ten days. I was therefor astonished to see him the next day in his correc place mounted upon a superb horse. When commented on this, he replied earnestly: "Sir when you receive an award from our Empero and King, you always keep a year's money i your belt to buy a horse on which you may b killed in His Majesty's service. If, in the cam paign ahead, I have the misfortune to lose m horse again, then I shall return to the depot t obtain another. The horse I am now riding bought yesterday with my own money from dragoon officer who no longer needs it for he has had his leg amputated."

"How much did it cost?"

"Twenty-five louis, sir." '

1799

When at the end of August Bonaparte left Egypt to return to France he took with him a detachment of 180 *Guides à cheval* and 125 *Guides à pied*. The men chosen were the most devoted veterans from each company. Soon after the *coup d'état* of 18 Brumaire the Guides, who had stayed in the South of France, were summoned to Paris and quartered in the *Caserne de Babylone*.

A decree of 28 November reorganized the *Garde du Directoire* as the *Garde des Consuls*, but it makes no mention of the Chasseurs.

1800

By a decree of 3 January a company of *Chasseurs à cheval* was created. Its commanding officer was Bonaparte's stepson Capt. Eugène de Beauharnais,

Detail of the colback ornament to which the plume was attached

who was promoted major on 5 March. The strength was 4 officers and 113 men, the latter being chosen from the Guides who had returned from Egypt, and 112 were veterans of the Italian campaign of 1796.

The cavalry of the *Garde Consulaire*, two squadrons of *Grenadiers à cheval* and the company of chasseurs, was commanded by *Chef de Brigade* Jean-Baptiste Bessières.

In May the company left Paris for Italy. It crossed the St Bernard Pass and was heavily engaged at the battle of Marengo (14 June) losing 70 out of its 115 horses. At the end of the campaign the corps returned to Paris. By a consular decree of 8 September it was augmented, becoming a squadron of two companies (troops) and 234 men.

1801

By a decree of 6 August the corps was increased to a headquarters and two squadrons. The staff was:–

Chef d'escadron	1
Adjutant-major	1
Porte-étendard	2
Brigadier-trompette	1
Maitres-ouvriers	4

At the end of September the remainder of the Guides got back from Egypt and were merged into the corps.

By a decree of 14 November the chasseurs became a Regiment. In theory the commanding officer was to be a *Chef de Brigade*, but in fact Bonaparte retained *Chef d'Éscadrons*, Beauharnais in command.

Job print of a Capitaine de l'état Major on the campaign of 1812. From the Bucquoy series

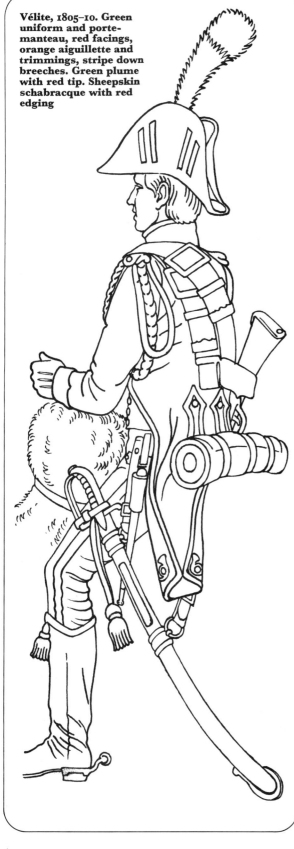

Vélite, 1805–10. Green uniform and portemanteau, red facings, orange aiguillette and trimmings, stripe down breeches. Green plume with red tip. Sheepskin schabracque with red edging

1802

By decree of 8 March the Headquarters was increased. It now included four standard-bearers, a trumpet-major, two trumpet corporals and a *timbalier* (kettle-drummer).

By decree of 1 October the Regiment was increased to four squadrons, with a total strength of 56 officers and 959 men. Beauharnais was promoted *Chef de Brigade* (13 October), and now had as his squadron commanders Morland, Nicolas Dahlmann, Frédéric-Auguste Beurmann and Hercule, a negro who had distinguished himself at Arcola in 1796.

1803

From 22 March, when summer training (*travail d'été*) began, the men were to parade on horseback every Monday and Thursday at 7.30 a.m. precisely on the Champ de Mars. Every Wednesday at the same hour they went through the foot exercise. In winter the parades seem to have been at 9.00 a.m. Swimming and rowing were among the exercises carried out in 1802 and 1803.

1804

By a decree of 21 January the Regiment was given a major who was to rank with the colonels of the line. The intrepid Morland was given this appointment. By the same decree the company of Mamelukes was attached to the Regiment.

By an Order of the Day of 18 May the *Garde des Consuls* became the *Garde Impériale*.

1805

On 13 May Beauharnais was made Viceroy of Italy, but he retained nominal command of the Regiment until about 1808. Morland now became the actual commanding officer with the title of *Colonel Commandant en second*, and Dahlmann was promoted Major.

On 17 September a Squadron of *vélites* (four companies) was created. It seems to have been intended as a kind of holding reinforcement unit.

The Regiment and the Mamelukes greatly distinguished themselves at the battle of Austerlitz (2 December), where two squadrons and the Mamelukes were led to the charge by Napoleon's senior A.D.C., Gen. Rapp, inflicting heavy casualties on the Russian Imperial Guard and capturing Prince Repnin, the commander of the Chevalier Guard.

At Austerlitz the Chasseurs suffered 19 officer casualties, including Colonel Morland, killed, and three squadron commanders wounded. Dahlmann now succeeded Morland, and Claude-Etienne Guyot became Major.

1806

The Regiment missed the battle of Jena (14 October), where the *1er Hussards* had the privilege of escorting the Emperor. The Chasseurs did, however, take part in Napoleon's triumphal entry into Berlin.

1807

At Eylau (8 February) the Regiment took part in Murat's great charge of 80 squadrons, which relieved the pressure on the French centre at the crisis of the battle. Seventeen of the officers were hit. In addition Dahlmann was mortally wounded. He had recently been promoted General (30 December 1806), but having no command he asked to be allowed to lead his old regiment and fell at their head. Major Guyot commanded the Regiment for the rest of the year, and Thiry was also promoted Major (16 February).

1808

On 18 January *Général de Brigade* Charles Lefèbvre-Desnöuettes replaced Dahlmann in command of the Regiment.

The Regiment was in Madrid when the populace rose on 2 May and eight of the officers, including Major Pierre Daumesnil, were wounded as well as five officers of the Mamelukes. The

Napoleon dressed in his favourite uniform of a Colonel of the Chasseurs, passes before the Opera House on his triumphal entry into Berlin

Regiment took part in General Montbrun's charge up the road at Somo-Sierra (30 November) but lost no officers for the Spanish gunners only managed to get off one salvo before the Polish and French cavalry got amongst them with the sabre. (This was the *second* charge, not the one in which the 3rd Squadron of the First Regiment of Polish *Chevau-Légers* was practically wiped out.)

On 28 November Napoleon, engaged in pressing the retreat of Sir John Moore towards Corunna, rode ahead of his army into the village of Valderas, which the British had quit but two hours previously. He was accompanied only by his staff and a squadron of the chasseurs. When Marshal Ney found that the Emperor had thus exposed himself he said to him: 'Sire, I thank Your Majesty for acting as my advance guard.' That it had been imprudent was proved next day (29 December) when General Lefèbvre-Desnöuettes caught up with the British rearguard, forded the River Esla and drove in their pickets, only to be rudely counter-attacked by Lord Paget (the Uxbridge of Waterloo fame), who led his men under cover

Guidon of 1802. Crimson with gold lettering and trimming. Hilpert

of the houses of Benavente to assail the French flank. Lefèbvre-Desnöuettes, wounded by a pistol shot, was taken prisoner. The Regiment had 6 other officers hurt and 2 captains taken, besides 55 chasseurs killed and wounded and 73 captured. To be outflanked and cut up in this fashion was a rude and novel experience for the Emperor's 'favourite children'.

The British cavalry who achieved this feat were the 10th Hussars with pickets of the 18th and the 3rd Hussars of the King's German Legion. Their losses amounted to no more than 50. It was this affair more than anything that convinced the Emperor that Moore had slipped from his clutches. It was time to return to France.

1809

The Regiment was at home again by the end of February. About this time it absorbed the *Chevau-légers* of the Grand-Duke of Berg, formerly the *Guides de Murat* (11 January) and the *Guides du Maréchal Mortier* (1 February).

On 5 June Major Guyot became *Colonel commandant en second*. Thiry was made *Général de Brigade* in the line, and, on the 13th, Daumesnil and Corbineau were promoted Major. At Wagram the Guard cavalry supported the right flank of Macdonald's great column which struck the decisive blow. The Regiment suffered at Wagram (6 July) having 5 officers killed and 10 wounded, including the two newly-promoted majors, each of whom lost a leg. Colonel Guyot was promoted *Général de brigade* (9 August), retaining the command, and Colonel Jean-Dieudonné Lion (14e Chasseurs) was brought in as third major of the corps.

1810

A quiet year! One officer wounded escorting prisoners in Spain.

1811

On 1 August the Regiment was increased to five squadrons and the *vélites* were done away with.

During the year squadrons were sent successively to serve with the divisions of the Garde in Spain. Guyot was promoted *Général de division*, but still retained the command. To replace Corbineau and

Napoleon at the Battle of Wagram, 6 July 1809. Painting by H. Vernet

Daumesnil as majors the Regiment received Colonel François d'Haugeranville (6 August) and Général Baron Exelmans (24 December).

1812

On 6 May General Lefèbvre-Desnöuettes, who had escaped by breaking his parole, returned from his captivity in England and resumed command of the Regiment.

The chasseurs, five squadrons and the company of Mamelukes, went through the Russian campaign, but though they lost 500 men, they only had two officers hit. At Borodino they had no officer casualties at all. But on 25 October, the day after the battle of Malojaroslavetz two squadrons, escorting the Emperor on a reconnaissance, were sharply engaged and had 4 officers wounded. A body of Cossacks appeared suddenly from a wood and charged straight at Napoleon. General Rapp and the escort managed to beat them off, but not before one had fought his way to within twenty yards of the Emperor. From this day forth, haunted by the fear of captivity, he always carried a bag of poison on a string about his neck.

The Regiment's losses in this campaign must on the whole be attributed not so much to the fighting as to the Russian climate.

1813

By a decree of 18 January the Regiment was increased to eight squadrons, each of 250 men, a total of 2,000. The three new squadrons were *Jeune Garde*.

On 6 March Lieutenant Charles Parquin (20th

Chasseurs) went out of curiosity to see a review at the Tuileries. Meeting Lefèbvre-Desnöuettes he asked to be allowed to join the Regiment, and, being recommended by Marshal Marmont, his commander in Spain, who arrived providentially while this interview was going on, was granted his request. His memoirs tell us much of the history of the Regiment during the next two years. He was fortunate in that Colonel Lion, who had been a captain in the 20th Chasseurs, was an old friend. Parquin was posted to the 10th Company, under Captain Klein de Kleinberg, an excellent officer, who was to be a general under the Bourbons, and was Lion's brother-in-law.

Grand Cross of the Order of Fidélité awarded to General Lefèbvre-Desnöuettes in 1807

The Regiment was, of course, at imperial reviews held at the Tuileries and elsewhere on occasions too numerous to name. At one (6 April 1813) Parquin, who wished to speak to Napoleon, posted himself on the left of an infantry regiment of the Young Guard 'since the Emperor did not spend much time with his *Guides* on these occasions and often galloped past them without stopping. . . .' On this occasion Parquin was able to state his services – eight campaigns, ten wounds, a colour taken from the enemy – and to secure the coveted cross of the Legion of Honour. His bold example encouraged two other officers also

returned from Spain, Goudmetz and Legout-Duplessis, and both approached the Emperor with success. Lieutenant Goudmetz had had two brothers killed in the service, and was to be wounded with the Regiment at Montmirail (11 February 1814); whilst Legout-Duplessis, as a sergeant of the 5th Dragoons, had broken among the Walloon Guards at Talavera, killing an officer and capturing the colour he bore.

> Napoleon (with a smile): *'A very fine exploit indeed, but who can confirm the truth of your story?'*
>
> Legout-Duplessis: *'Your aide-de-camp, General Corbineau, who is with you now, Sire, was colonel of the regiment at the time and it was he who led the charge.'*

A nod from General Corbineau[1] settled the matter. Can one wonder that with officers of this stamp the story of the Chasseurs is one of almost unbroken success? Or that they would follow a master who knew so well how to foster their loyalty?

Parquin throws an interesting light on the escort duties performed by the Regiment.

'Between the 20th and the 30th of May I and my troop were part of the squadron of chasseurs (who were more frequently known as *guides* when in the field), which was directly under the Emperor's orders. In wartime the Emperor always had at his disposal four squadrons drawn from the different arms of the Old Guard cavalry; these he could throw against the enemy if the need arose. The squadron of chasseurs had a special task. A lieutenant, a sergeant, two corporals, twenty-two chasseurs and a trumpeter rode in front of and behind the Emperor. A corporal and four chasseurs galloped ahead of the Emperor and cleared a way for him. One of the chasseurs carried his despatch case and another his field-glass. If the Emperor stopped and dismounted, these chasseurs would immediately do likewise, fix their bayonets to their carbines and move about in a square with the Emperor in the centre of it. The officer commanding the escort troop followed him constantly. Only Murat and the Prince de Neufchâtel had precedence over this officer.

'If the Emperor took quarters in a house, this officer occupied the room nearest to that of the

Emperor. The chasseurs in the escort troop dismounted and stood holding their horses in front of the house occupied by the Emperor, who always had one of his own horses held in readiness there by two grooms. This troop was relieved every two hours so that the same arrangements held good whatever the time of day or night. The first person the Emperor saw on leaving his rooms was the officer in charge of the escort. It was a post of great honour and responsibility. This body of men was entirely devoted to the Emperor and was, moreover, well rewarded for its devotion. In each troop there were four chasseurs who received not only the cross of the *Légion d'honneur* and the cross of the *Couronne de Fer* with its income of 250 francs, but also dividends from the canal companies or the Mont de Milan which brought them between 500 and 800 francs.'

On the lighter side he tells us something of the customs of the Guard. For example it was a

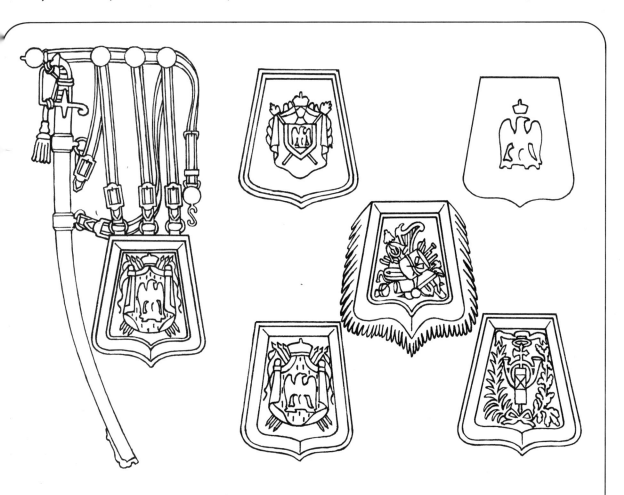

SABRETACHES

Left: Officer's sabre and sabretache. This example was exhibited at the *Exposition retrospective militaire* of 1900

Top left: Empire. Full-dress sabretache of a chasseur of 1900

Top right: Full dress sabretache of a chasseur of the 2nd Regiment, 1815. Black leather with gold ornaments

Centre: Sabretache of the kettle-drummer, Bruno Lemoine, 1805–6. Gold ornaments on a crimson background. From the Musée de l'Armée, Paris

Bottom left: Empire. Trooper's sabretache

Bottom right: Consulate. Trooper's sabretache. This example from the Museum at Colmar has the legend GARDE DES CONSULS in the scroll at the top

A chasseur escort holds the horse of a staff-officer on reconnaissance. From a painting by Meissonier

longstanding custom of the officers to assemble at the *Hotel de l'Écu*[2] whenever they passed through Epernay. 'There they would dine together and drink the health of the Emperor in the best champagne.'

Lion was promoted *Général de Brigade* on 21 June but remained in command.

The regiment saw a good deal of fighting in 1813 sustaining 26 officer casualties, seven of them at Leipzig (18 October). At the end of the year the Old Guard (General Lion) and the Young Guard squadrons (Colonel Meuziau) separated, the former staying with the Grand Army and the latter going to Belgium, where, under Lefèbvre-Desnöuettes, they played their part in the defence of Antwerp.

Lion's command consisted of the first five squadrons; the 11th Company of the 6th Squadron

(Capt. Parquin) and the Mamelukes. At the end of the year (1 December) Guyot went to command the *Grenadiers à cheval*.

1814

The Regiment played a gallant part in the campaign of France, and fourteen of its officers were killed or wounded. Of its many exploits the charge of Parquin and his squadron at St Dizier (20 March) serves well to demonstrate the *élan* of this magnificent corps.

'I was riding with my men at the head of the column when the general came and ordered me to charge, regardless of cost, with my squadron against eighteen cannon which the Russians had sited in the open. I obeyed the order immediately, but when we were a hundred yards from the guns the enemy grape-shot so decimated the ranks of my squadron that I gave the order to the two right-hand troops and to the two left-hand troops to attack in extended order so as to be less exposed. Soon the *lanciers rouges* of the Guard arrived and after their charge we seized the guns.

'A division of Russian cuirassiers, which came rushing to the help of their gunners, clashed with the lancers, who received the timely support of the 3rd and the 6th Dragoons under General Milhaud[3]. Together they routed the enemy heavy cavalry, taking nearly 600 prisoners. In this close combat I unseated a Russian sergeant with a thrust from my sabre at his neck. . . .'

Of this action General Sébastiani[4] observed to the Emperor:

'I have been a cavalry officer for twenty-five years and I do not ever remember seeing a more brilliant charge than the one carried out by your leading squadron.'

At the end of the campaign the Regiment numbered 89 officers and 1,357 men.

On the Restoration of the Bourbons the Regiment and the first company of Mamelukes became, by a royal decree of 14 May, the *Corps Royal des Chasseurs à Cheval de France*. At the same time the Young Guard squadrons were broken up and distributed among the 2nd, 3rd and 7th Chasseurs.

By an *ordonnance* of 26 June 1814 the establishment of the Regiment was fixed at four squadrons each of two companies. The strength was reduced to 44 officers and 641 men. Lefèbvre-Desnöuettes retained the command with General Lion as Major.

1815

When the Emperor Napoleon returned from Elba the Imperial Guard was re-established by a decree of 21 March. The Regiment was given its old name, and 412 former chasseurs and 94 Mamelukes, who had been discharged the previous year, returned to the corps.

A new unit the *2e Régiment de Chasseurs à cheval de la Jeune Garde* was created by decree of 15 May. It was not ready in time to take the field with the Army of the North. Its major and commanding officer was *Maréchal du Camp* Merlin-de-Douai.

In their last battle, Waterloo (18 June), the Chasseurs of the Old Guard suffered severely. In the early phases Lefèbvre-Desnöuettes with the Light Cavalry of the Guard was in comparative safety in support of the French right wing, in rear of Milhaud's division of cuirassiers and to the right rear of D'Erlon's Corps. The Regiment probably did not go into action until about 4.00 p.m. By this time Marshal Ney had massed not less than 5,000 French cavalry opposite Wellington's centre. As is well known Ney launched his

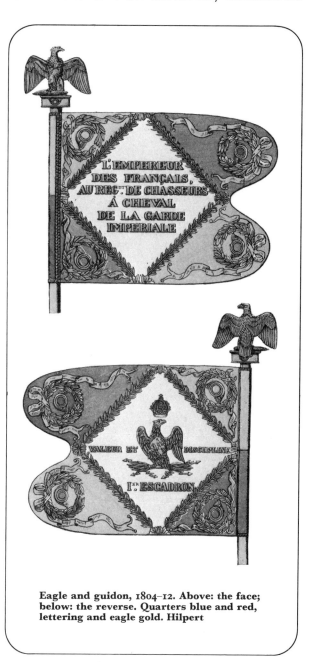

Eagle and guidon, 1804–12. Above: the face; below: the reverse. Quarters blue and red, lettering and eagle gold. Hilpert

cavalry without infantry support against the Allied squares. Lefèbvre-Desnöuettes seems to have sent his men in on his own initiative in order to support Milhaud: or it may be that his men surged forward spontaneously: it certainly seems that the Red Lancers did. The French cavalry, on the evidence of their foes, behaved nobly, but they could make little impression upon infantry in squares. In the charges that followed the Regiment lost 20 officers, including five killed and one mortally wounded.

Those who survived the disaster at Waterloo took part in the retreat to the Loire, and eventually the Regiment was disbanded at Périgueux early in November.

Few indeed of the chasseurs served on under the Bourbons. They, and the Guides before them, had followed Napoleon Bonaparte from Arcola to Waterloo, by way of the Pyramids, Marengo, Austerlitz and a score of other famous fields. They remained loyal to him in his last exile.

Let a Frenchman, Commandant Bucquoy, who devoted his talents to the history of the Grand Army have the last word:

'Mais si les Chasseurs à cheval de la Garde imperiale restaient fidèles au souvenir de leur Empereur, lui de son côté ne les oubliait pas, et il allait leur rendre après sa mort un suprême hommage, ayant revêtu leur légendaire frac vert pour descendre au cercueil et entrer avec lui dans l'immortalité.'

Personalities

'None of these fine men was lacking in gratitude towards his Emperor.'
'Napoleon . . . was well aware of the devotion of his guides. . . .'

CHARLES PARQUIN

The senior officers of the regiment included, at one time or another, a number of distinguished generals. Men such as these set the tone of a corps and that is what gives interest to their individual records of service.

BESSIÈRES, JEAN-BAPTISTE, DUC D'ISTRIE (1768–1813), Marshal of France. Captain of grenadiers in the National Guard of Prayssac, 1789. Chosen by Bonaparte after the affair of Cremona to command his company of Guides, 5 June 1796, and made provisional *Chef d'Éscadrons* on the battlefield of Roveredo, 4 September 1796. Distinguished himself at Rivoli (14 January) and La Favorita (16 January) and was sent to Paris with the Austrian colours taken on these occasions. Promoted *Chef de Brigade* (9 March 1797) and commanded the Guides of the Army of the Orient

Top: Kettle-drum

Bottom: Kettle-drum, 1810. Crimson with gold fringes, imperial crown, eagle and wreaths. The eagle has a blue background. The motto in the scroll is HONNEUR/ET PATRIE. Dubois de l'Estang Collection

Marshal Jean-Baptiste Bessières

(1798–9), returning to France with Bonaparte and assisting him in the *coup d'état* of the 18th Brumaire. Fought at Marengo (1800) and became commander-in-chief of the cavalry of the Consular Guard, 20 November 1801. General of division, 1802. Marshal of the Empire and Grand Officer of the Legion of Honour, 1804. Colonel-General commanding the cavalry of the Imperial Guard, 20 July 1804. Grand Eagle of the Legion of Honour and Commander of the Couronne de Fer, 1805. Fought at Austerlitz, Jena, Eylau and Friedland. For his loyal services Napoleon loaded him with honours and money. He defeated Don Gregorio de la Cuesta, a very indifferent general, at Medina del Rio Seco, 14 July 1808. After being with Napoleon during his brief Spanish campaign he remained there to command the northern provinces, until recalled to take part in the Austrian campaign of 1809. Created Duke of Istria. Received a contusion in the thigh at Wagram. Assumed command of the Imperial Guard, 19 January 1809. Commanded the Army of the North in Spain, 15 January–*c.* September 1811

Brass ornaments from the saddlery of the Corps

and fought under Masséna at Fuentes de Oñoro, where the French were repulsed by Wellington (5 May). Took command of the cavalry of the Imperial Guard, 5 May 1812, and served in Russia. Killed outright by a cannon ball at Rippach near Weissenfels, 1 May 1813.

The Regiment's senior officers included many others of distinction. The career of Eugène de Beauharnais, Viceroy of Italy, is too well known to require description here. The careers of others who did not achieve general rank are unfortunately somewhat obscure. Among these must be included the gallant Colonel Morland who was killed at Austerlitz, and Hercule the negro lieutenant who was already in Bonaparte's Guides during the Italian Campaign.

NICOLAS DAHLMANN (1769–1807), Morland's successor, originally enlisted as an *enfant de troupe* in the cavalry regiment of Dauphin in 1777 and, surprisingly enough, was paid with effect from 9 September 1777 when he had not yet reached the ripe old age of 8. Truly the workings of the army of the Ancièn Règime were sometimes astonishing. He joined the Guides on 22 June 1796, served in Italy and Egypt and was nominated lieutenant on the field of battle at Salahieh on 12 August 1798. He returned to France with Bonaparte as a captain, becoming a *Chef d'Éscadrons* in 1802 and an officer of *Légion d'honneur* in 1804. He fought at Austerlitz and Jena; was promoted *Général de Brigade* on 30 December 1806, and succumbed to a grapeshot wound in the right thigh, received at Eylau.

FRÉDÉRIC-AUGUSTE, BARON DE BEURMANN (1777–1815) was another *enfant de troupe* who served in the Salm-Salm infantry, receiving half pay from 10 August 1784. In 1788, when he was nearly 11 he was admitted as a soldier of the same regiment on full pay. In 1792 he was commissioned and his early service was in the Armies of the North, the Sambre-et-Meuse, Danube, and Helvetia where he was ADC to Mortier. After further service in the Army of the Rhine he was posted to the *Chasseurs à cheval* of the Consular Guard, 20 November 1800. He received two bayonet wounds at Austerlitz and was made colonel of the 17th

Dragoons early in 1806. He afterwards served in Spain. He won the Legion of Honour and the Order of Military Merit. He retired at his own request on 27 January 1815 and blew his brains out on 13 April following.

LAUDE-ETIENNE, BARON (LATER COUNT) GUYOT (1768–1837), enlisted as a soldier in the *Chasseurs à cheval de Bretagne* on 1 November 1790 and was commissioned in 1793 serving in Vendée, Italy and Germany. He was posted to the *Chasseurs à cheval* of the Consular Guard as a captain on 13 October 1802, becoming *Chef d'Éscadrons* in 1804 and Major just after Austerlitz. He fought at Eylau. Became a colonel in the Guard on 16 February 1807; obtained a gift of 10,000 francs per annum from the funds of Westphalia and was made a baron in 1808. The same year he served under Napoleon in Spain and was made Knight of the *Couronne de Fer d'Italie*. He fought at Essling and Wagram, was promoted *Général de Brigade* and received another 20,000 francs from Swedish

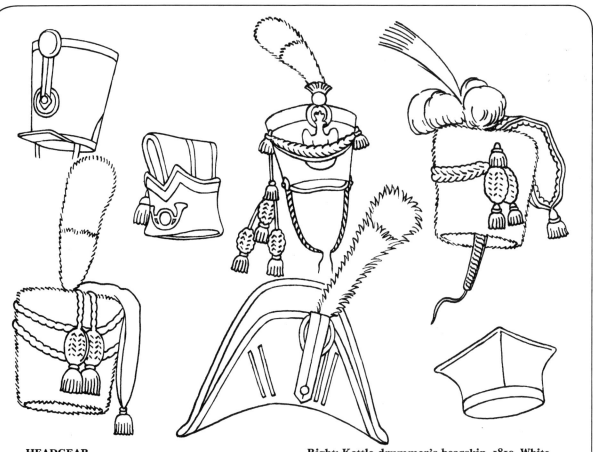

HEADGEAR

Top left: 2nd Regiment, 1815. Chasseur's full-dress shako. Scarlet with yellow pompom and trimmings. Black peak and *couvre-nuque*

Left centre: Trooper's *Bonnet de police*, 1813. Worn for undress parades, such as stables, exercising young horses' or swimming training. Green with orange horn and trimmings and a dark red stripe above the deep orange band above the bugle-horn

Right centre: Chasseur. Squadrons of the Young Guard, 1813–14. Scarlet, with orange trimming, black peak and gold eagle. Scarlet pompom; plume green at the bottom and scarlet at the top. Musée de l'Armée.

Right: Kettle-drummer's bearskin, 1810. White with gold lace. Scarlet busby-bag. White aigrette with crimson plumage at its base. Dubois de l'Estang Collection

Bottom left: Trumpeter's full-dress busby, 1804–5. The bearskin is white with gold lace, and crimson busby-bag. The lower part of the plume is crimson and the upper part is white. After Hoffmann

Centre: Chasseur's bicorne, 1803–4. Walking-out dress. Black with orange trimmings, green plume with red tip. Regimental Order Book

Right: Officer's undress cap. 2nd Regiment, 1815

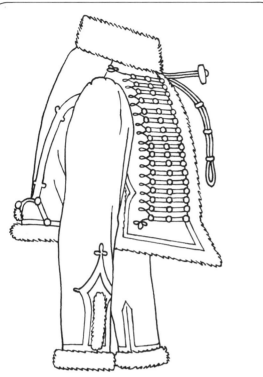

Chasseur. Pelisse of scarlet cloth, trimmed with black lambskin, for winter dress

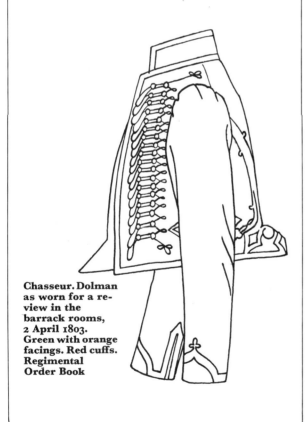

Chasseur. Dolman as worn for a review in the barrack rooms, 2 April 1803. Green with orange facings. Red cuffs. Regimental Order Book

Pomerania. 1809 was therefore a good year for him! Things continued to go well; in 1810 another 10,000 francs came his way from Galicia. In 1811 he became Chamberlain to the Emperor, Commander of the *Légion d'honneur* and general of division. He commanded the Chasseurs of the Guard in Russia in 1812. He was wounded at Lutzen on 2 May 1813, but not badly for he also served at Bautzen on 20/21 May 1813 and was made a count soon after. He was taken prisoner at Kulm on 30 August but exchanged in time for the Battle of Leipzig. Transferred to the *Grenadiers à cheval de la Garde*, he served in the Campaign of France 1814 and received two bullet wounds at Waterloo. He retired in 1816 but was re-employed from 1830–33.

NICOLAS-MARIN, BARON THIRY (1769–1827), began his military career as a *cannonier* in the regiment of *Grenoble Artillerie* on 2 August 1786 and was commissioned in 1792. He distinguished himself when he and a party of the 10th Hussars, belonging to the Army of the North, captured two howitzers and their crews in an affair at Blaton on 18 August 1793. He again did well at Quiberon on 17 June 1795 and won a sabre of honour in 1802. He joined the *Chasseurs de la Garde* as a *Chef d'Éscadrons* on 15 September 1805. He was seriously wounded with two bayonet thrusts in the stomach at Austerlitz and bruised on the left leg by a cannon ball at Eylau. Promoted Major in 1807 he, like Guyot, came in for plenty of decorations and monetary grants. He was given a light cavalry brigade in 1809. During his later service he received three wounds at Borodino but, after this time, his career was undistinguished.

CHARLES, COUNT LEFÈBVRE-DESNÖUETTES (1773–1822), son of a cloth merchant, he escaped from college to join an infantry regiment, but three times his parents bought his discharge. Eventually he became a chasseur in the Oratoire battalion of the Paris National Guard on 1 December 1789. He was commissioned in 1793. He fought at Marengo in 1800 and at Austerlitz in 1805 winning the Legion of Honour. In 1806 he became a general of brigade. Much money and many honours came his way. He won the battle of Tudela in Spain on 7 June 1808 and was made general of division. He fought at Somo-sierra and was commanding the *Chasseurs de la Garde* when they were routed by the English cavalry at Benevente on 29 December 1808. Wounded by a pistol bullet, he was captured and taken to England. He escaped in 1812, having broken his parole, and resumed command of the regiment, serving in Russia. Wounded at Winkowo on 18 October 1812, he left the army at Smorgoni with the Emperor to return to Paris. He served in Germany in 1813 and was given command of the cavalry of the Jeune Garde on 25 November. He served throughout the campaign of France, despite two bayonet wounds at Brienne on 29 January 1814, and commanded Napoleon's escort after his abdication. Hearing of Napoleon's return from Elba he went to Cambrai where his regiment was in garrison and led them in an unsuccessful attempt to seize the arsenal at La Fère. Napoleon, on reaching Paris, made him colonel of the Chasseurs of the Imperial Guard on 14 April 1815 and a peer of France on 2 June. He commanded the light cavalry division of the Guard at Waterloo. Upon the return of the Bourbons he was proscribed and took refuge in the United States. In 1822 he was drowned when the ship in which he was returning to Europe was wrecked off Kinsale on 22 April. In tribute to his memory, his widow erected a remarkable lighthouse, of decidedly phallic appearance, on the coast off which he perished.

PIERRE, BARON DAUMESNIL (1777–1832) enlisted as a trooper in the *22ᵉ Chasseurs à cheval* on 15 March 1794 and became a corporal in Bonaparte's Guides in Italy on 13 June 1797. He served with the Army of the Orient and was wounded by a sabre cut at the unsuccessful assault on Acre and was hurled from the top of the ramparts into the ditch by the explosion of a mine. He twice saved the life of General Bonaparte and carried off the standard of the Captain Pasha at Aboukir on 25 July 1799. He returned to France with Bonaparte and was posted to the Chasseurs of the Consular Guard and commissioned in 1800. He served with the Grand Army from 1805 to 1807, in Spain in 1808 and in Germany in 1809. He was wounded in the left leg at Wagram and it had to be amputated. He had become an officer of the *Légion*

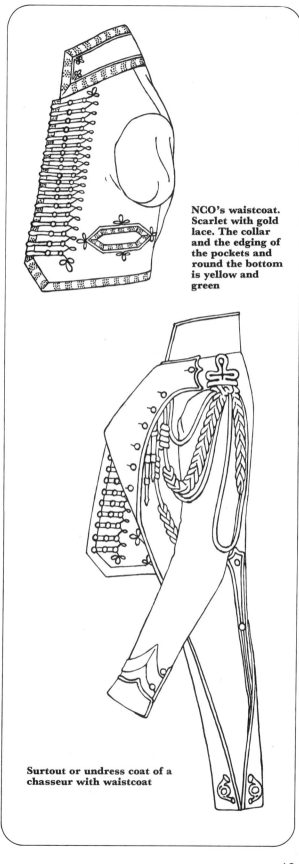

NCO's waistcoat. Scarlet with gold lace. The collar and the edging of the pockets and round the bottom is yellow and green

Surtout or undress coat of a chasseur with waistcoat

d'honneur in 1806 and received several monetary grants, whilst in 1810 he became a baron. In 1812 he was made general of brigade. In 1814 he was commandant of the fortress of Vincennes and, on the night of 30/31 March after the battle on the heights before Paris, he collected all the abandoned *matèriel* on the battlefield and took it into his fortress and thereafter refused to surrender. He was once more governor of Vincennes in 1815 when he defied Blücher, and again in 1830 when he refused to deliver the place to the insurgents against Charles X's government. Promoted Lieutenant-General in 1831, he did not live long to enjoy it because he was carried off by the cholera epidemic of 1832.

JEAN-DIEUDONNÉ, BARON – LATER COUNT – LION (1771 to 1840) was born at Walcourt in Belgium where, in 1688,[5] the British Army had defeated the French. Lion enlisted in the Royal-Liègeois on 10 September 1789 and was commissioned in 1794. At Mainburg on 7 September 1796 he captured an Austrian battalion with two cannons and a colour. He saw much action and was wounded several times and, on 10 August 1809, he was made Colonel-Major of the *Chasseurs à cheval de la Garde*. On 20 April 1809 he captured two colours and two battalions of Hungarians with his regiment, the 2nd Chasseurs. He was made a baron in 1810 and served in Russia in 1812 and Saxony in 1813, being promoted general of brigade but continuing to command the Chasseurs of the Guard. At Vauchamps on 14 February 1814 he received two bullet wounds, one in the head and the other in the right hand. He refused to join in Lefèbvre-Desnöuettes' rising at Cambrai on 11 March 1815 and followed Louis XVIII into exile. In consequence he continued to enjoy a distinguished military career under the Restoration, most of his later commands being in the gendarmerie.

FRANÇOIS-CHARLES-JEAN-PIERRE-MARIE D'AVRANGES, BARON D'HAUGERANVILLE (1782–1817), son of a general and nephew of Marshal Berthier, enlisted in the 5th Hussars on 17 October 1796 and was commissioned in 1800. He joined the Chasseurs of the Consular Guard the following year but was posted as a captain to the 9th Dragoons in 1802. After service in the great campaigns of the Grand Army, 1805 to 1807, and in

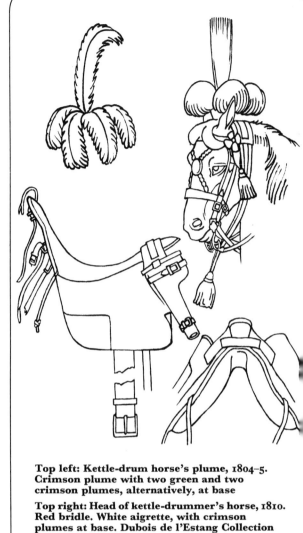

Top left: Kettle-drum horse's plume, 1804–5. Crimson plume with two green and two crimson plumes, alternatively, at base

Top right: Head of kettle-drummer's horse, 1810. Red bridle. White aigrette, with crimson plumes at base. Dubois de l'Estang Collection

Bottom left: Corporal's saddle

Bottom right: Corporal's saddle, back view. Eduouard Detaille's Collection, Musée de l'Armée

the Austrian Campaign of 1809 where he receive a bullet wound in the left leg at Wagram, he wa made major of the *Chasseurs à cheval de la Garde* c 6 August 1811. He fought at Borodino and wa made general of brigade on 27 February 1813. H did not serve with the Guard thereafter. He wa wounded and captured at Leipzig and was co valescent in 1814 and followed the King to Ghe in 1815, commanding his military househo during the campaign in Belgium – not that it d anything.

Prince Eugene de Beauharnais, Commander of the *Chasseurs à cheval*

Naturally, though the senior officers of the regiment may set its tone, without good junior officers, NCOs and chasseurs, the regiment would never have been a *corps d'elite*. The quality of these last lives on in the pages of Parquin. Though there is not room in this book to quote long passages from his memoirs, they are among the liveliest of the many which have come down to us from Napoleonic days.

Uniforms of the Consular Guard

The Consular Guard, organized early in 1800, was to escort the First Consul wherever he went. Yet many of the Guides, newly returned from Egypt, were in rags. It was a question of reclothing the whole company of *Chasseurs à cheval*. It was, therefore, possible to make innovations. The new uniform is preserved for us in Isabey's painting *Revue de Decadi*. Beauharnais the commanding officer has rich trappings of an oriental style, but those of the other officers and the men follow the regulations of 1791.

The Chasseurs of the Consular Guard wore the colback, a fur busby such as hussars had sometimes worn during the eighteenth century, which by 1800 had replaced the *bicorne* worn by the Guides of 1796. Whether this was adopted in Egypt or rather later is not absolutely certain, but it was worn at Marengo.

THE HUSSAR UNIFORM

When, after Marengo, the Guides were increased in number their uniform became more elaborate,

and although chasseurs they were ordered a hussar uniform – *habillement à la hussarde* (8 September 1800).

	Francs
1 shako[1] and plume	24
1 pelisse of scarlet cloth	45
1 dolman of green cloth	30
1 *bonnet de police*[2]	8.84
1 pair, shoes	4.75
1 pair, black gaiters	5
1 shirt	5
1 *col noir en soie*[3]	2
1 hat, maroon pompom and cockade	8.75
1 pair of stockings	2.5
1 pair of scarlet breeches[4]	25
1 sabretache	24
1 green cloth schabraque trimmed with scarlet cloth with '*glands, galon et cor de chasse*'	50

[1] This was the fur colback with a small peak (*colbàck à visière*).
[2] Forage cap is perhaps the best translation.
[3] Black silk stock or neckcloth.
[4] These were not overalls but the type worn with boots.

Most of these articles were expected to last three years, and should therefore have been in use until the end of 1803, but the Regiment was increased to four squadrons in October 1802 and so it would

Belt, sash and trousers or *hongroise* of undress uniform

Detail of a painting by Meissonier showing the escort of chasseurs (left) at the Battle of Friedland

not be surprising if changes in the uniform came in at that time. It is likely that the third type of colback, the one which the Regiment wore throughout the Empire, was introduced at this date.

While the full-dress was *à la hussarde* the undress (*deuxième tenue*) of the earlier chasseur style remained in use.

Certain items of clothing scarcely altered throughout the Empire.

Colback. Bearskin. Under the Consulate there was at first no pompom, but later, perhaps, each squadron had one of a special colour. Each chasseur had a waterproof cover for his colback made of black cloth, waxed and varnished.

Bicorne hat. Black felt.

Bonnet de police. Green cloth.

Dolman. Green *à la hussarde* with scarlet facings. Five rows each of 18 buttons, those in the centre being large and the rest medium.

Pelisse. Scarlet, lined with white flannel, trimmed with black lambskin, and decorated with 24 big and 72 medium-sized buttons.

Waistcoat No. 1 (*Gilet tressé*). Scarlet. With three rows of 18 little buttons for the men and five rows for the NCOs. This waistcoat was worn with the coat or under the pelisse.

Waistcoat No. 2 (*Gilet croisé*). Red cloth without sleeves, ornamented with two rows of buttons.

Belt. The belt was not made in one rigid piece but consisted of a series of more-or-less overlapping links.

Coat (*Habit*). Green cloth with pointed turnbacks (*revers*), ornamented with hunting horns embroidered in orange (*aurore*) cloth. The coat had 24 big buttons and 6 small. On the right an orange (*aurore*) shoulder-knot (*trèfle*), backed with scarlet was worn, and on the left shoulder orange aiguillettes.

Stable jacket (*Veste d'écurie*).[6] Green jersey.[7] It probably conformed to the regulations of 1791 and had 20 buttons in two rows. This was certainly the case after 1812.

Hongroise. Green breeches ornamented with orange (*aurore*) cloth.

23

Overalls (*Pantalon du cheval*). Green cloth with leather on the inside of the leg, with a red cloth stripe, and 18 buttons on each leg.

Trousers for fatigues (*Pantalon du treillis*). Ornamented with 36 bone buttons.

Boots (*A la hussarde*). With orange (*aurore*) ornaments.

Gaiters. Black, of the general pattern used throughout the army. Worn with shoes, over the *hongroise* or under the *pantalon du treillis*, for foot parades and stables.

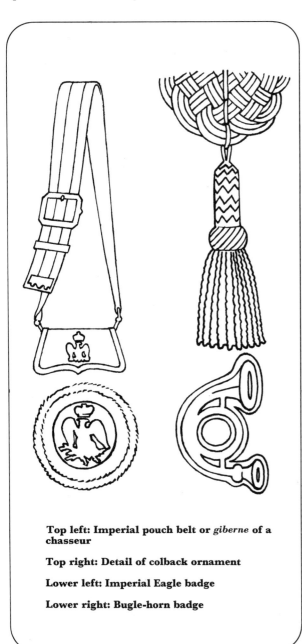

Top left: Imperial pouch belt or *giberne* of a chasseur

Top right: Detail of colback ornament

Lower left: Imperial Eagle badge

Lower right: Bugle-horn badge

Conductors' uniform. An inventory of 1 April 1812 records green waistcoats, greatcoats and *pantalons de charretiers* which, doubtless, were intended for the men in charge of the vehicles of the Regiment.

TRUMPETERS AND KETTLE-DRUMMERS

In Egypt the trumpeters of the Guides had a sky-blue uniform with crimson facings. In full dress (*grande tenue*) they continued to wear leather breeches as under the Old Régime.

When under the Consulate the unit received colbacks, those issued to the trumpeters were of white fur. At the end of 1800 the trumpeters received the hussar uniform. Items which were green for the Chasseurs were sky blue for the trumpeters, and those that were scarlet for the former were crimson for the latter. On any crimson clothing the trumpeters wore gold lace backed with blue cloth, and on blue articles they had gold lace backed with crimson cloth, except of course on the collar and turnbacks where the insignia was just gold.

Kettle-drummer. By 8 March 1802 the unit had a *timbalier* a very young man named Bruno Lemoine who had entered the Consular Guard as a musician at the age of 14. Because of his small stature Bonaparte made him the kettle-drummer of the Chasseurs, and had a Mameluke costume made for him.

LES CAHIERS DE MALMAISON

Ten of the Order Books of Eugène Beauharnais as commanding officer of the Chasseurs of the Guard have survived. They cover the period February 1800 to 31 October 1804. Up to 1 October 1802 they relate to all the cavalry of the Guard and are signed by Bessières and Michel Ordener (1755–1811), the commander of the *Grenadiers à cheval*, as well as Beauharnais. Thereafter they are only concerned with the chasseurs. They have a certain amount to say about dress. For example, men who had received arms of honour were to carry them on all occasions except parades in barracks (*service de quartier*). Boots were always to be worn with walking-out dress (*tenue de ville*).

Lieutenant, Standard Bearer, Full Dress 1808

A

Trumpeter, Full Dress 1803

MICHAEL YOU

Chasseur 1805–14, Full Dress as worn on service escort duty

Full Dress under the Consulate.

1 Chasseur, 1800;

2 Chef de brigade Eugène de Beauharnais, 1800;

3 Officer, Consulate

1

2

3

D

Walking-out Dress.
1 Chasseur, 1803–4,
Sundays in winter;
2 Officer, 1804;
3 Chasseur, 1803–4, week-
days in winter

E

On active service.

1 Chasseur, Battle of Austerlitz, 1805;

2 Chasseur, campaign of 1806, escort duty on foot;

3 Chasseur, campaigns of 1806 and 1807, mounted escort duty

1

2

3

On active service.
1 Officer, 1812–14, on the march;
2 Officer, 1808, Somo-sierra;
3 Chasseur, 1808, on the march in Spain

G

1 **Chef de musique**, 1810
2 **Kettle-drummer**, 1805;
3 **Trumpeter**, 1801;

The sabretache was never to be worn except with the *tenue à la hussarde*, that is to say pelisse and dolman. This was the usual thing with Hussar regiments.

The hair was to be worn in uniform fashion with a queue six inches long (9 July 1800). Bessières issued elaborate orders on the subject on 18 April 1811. He himself continued to wear the queue until the day of his death in 1813, by which time it was certainly very outmoded among general officers.

The Chasseurs with pelisse, dolman, coat, stable-jacket, three forms of waistcoat and three different headgears, not to mention breeches, overalls and so forth, had a number of different orders of dress. It is thanks to the Cahiers de la Malmaison that we are able to sort them out.

Full Dress (*Grande Tenue*). Although artists habitually show us the Chasseurs in this order of dress it was in fact rarely worn.

Escort and Picket Order (*Tenue d'Éscorte et de Piquet*). By an order of 11 October 1803 it was

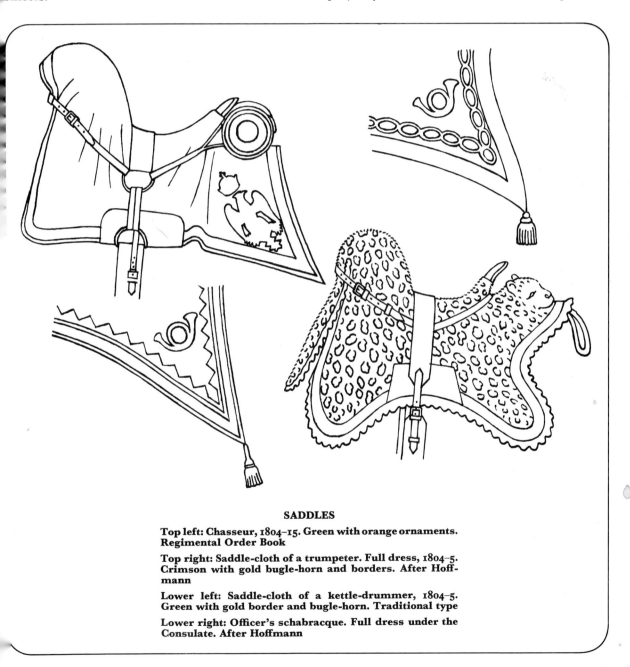

SADDLES

Top left: Chasseur, 1804–15. Green with orange ornaments. Regimental Order Book

Top right: Saddle-cloth of a trumpeter. Full dress, 1804–5. Crimson with gold bugle-horn and borders. After Hoffmann

Lower left: Saddle-cloth of a kettle-drummer, 1804–5. Green with gold border and bugle-horn. Traditional type

Lower right: Officer's schabracque. Full dress under the Consulate. After Hoffmann

laid down that from the 23rd mounted pickets should wear the pelisse, leather breeches, *gilet tressé*, belt, sabretache, colback, etc. After 6.00 p.m. they were allowed to wear overalls. Only in foul weather were the men allowed to put the waterproof covers over their colbacks. The point is that in the summer the chasseurs wore the dolman and in the winter the pelisse. Bucquoy points out that the Emperor's escort entered Vienna in 1809 and Moscow in 1812 wearing the dolman. Though the men had green cloaks, the escort were forbidden to wear them, the idea being that one could tell at a glance from its distinctive uniforms that the staff that was approaching was that of the Emperor in person.

Cape (*Manteau*). The Chasseurs of the Consular Guard had a cloak called '*Trois-quart*' without sleeves and with a very short cape. At the end of the consulate a new model was issued (*c.* February 1804) with a larger cape. The capes were to be worn outside the cloaks when on the march, for foot duties, and in foul weather when escorting the First Consul, during which service the cloak was never to be worn.

The Chasseurs liked to wear this convenient garment when walking out in wet weather, but soon this was expressly forbidden (17 February 1804).

Here are examples of the orders for dismounted inspections:

3 *Fructidor an XI* (21 August 1803)
Revue de propreté à 9 heures. Troupe: hongroise verte, gilet tressé, colback et plumet, fourniment, sabre et carabines. Les officiers aurent le chapeau et le plumet, le pantalon rouge et le gilet blanc sans giberne.

A charming picture by François Flameng of a chasseur in conversation with two ladies in the Consulate period

(Inspection at 0900 hours. **Men:** green breeches, full-dress waistcoat, colback and plume. Sabres and carbines. **Officers:** Hat and plume, red breeches and white waistcoats. No cartridge-cases.)

15 *Floréal an XII* (5 May 1804)
La troupe sera en dolman, pantalon de nankin, gilet blanc, chapeau et plumet, sabre et sabretache. Les officiers aurent la même tenue, à l'exception de la sabretache.

(The men will wear the dolman, nankeen pantaloons, white waistcoats, hat and plume, sabre and sabretache. The officers will be in the same *tenue*, except for the sabretache.)

NCOs. Generally speaking the NCOs wore the same uniform as the men, the main difference being that their badges of rank were in gold.

Officers. Officers' aiguillettes and badges of every sort, were also, of course, in gold, and they wore an epaulette on the left shoulder and an aiguillette on the right. Their pelisses were trimmed with light grey fur. The officers of the Regimental Headquarters were distinguished from those of the squadrons by their white plumes.

All the officers, including Bessières and Beauharnais, seem to have had a liking for scarlet breeches. Some also went in for red or green boots, which was hardly regulation – rather what the French call *tenue de fantaisie*.

A portrait of Lieutenant Bourdon preserves the *tenue* worn in society: white silk stockings, buckled shoes, white waistcoat and breeches, a dress sword and a bicorne hat (*le chapeau claque*): in short the legendary uniform of the First Consul.

Servants and grooms. A certain number of officers' servants were allowed (Order of 26 February 1803) so long as they had good conduct certificates. They were compelled to wear a simple green uniform coat, and a three-cornered hat. Waistcoats and trousers were not of any obligatory colour. The servants were not allowed to bear arms. Since Beauharnais gave notice that he meant to inspect the servants himself, one may assume that these orders were adhered to. Senior officers and those who were well-to-do, having several horses, naturally required grooms and could afford to dress their servants with *un*

Officer's cloak as worn on campaign, 1813

peu plus de luxe, and this Beauharnais' orders permitted.

ARMAMENT

SABRE. All ranks were armed with the sabre. The 1802 model was issued on 21 September 1802.

CARBINE. The Guides returned from Egypt with a variety of different carbines. Though they were supposed to have that of 1786, they actually had cut down muskets, foreign carbines and even blunderbusses. In 1800 carbines of the 1786 pattern were issued, and on 13 October 1803 a new model which had a socket for fixing the bayonet. A white leather bayonet frog was issued.

PISTOL. Corporals and Chasseurs carried one pistol in their left holster. NCOs and trumpeters, having no carbines, had two pistols. Quartermasters and corporals had small axes which were carried in the right-hand holster. These were only carried on the march.

SABRETACHE. Details of the patterns in use are shown on page 11.

GIBERNE. The cartridge-case of black leather was probably ornamented with a metal horn.

SADDLERY. At first the saddle was of the normal light cavalry pattern, which was intended to be covered by a schabraque. However, as time went by the Chasseurs received the first light cavalry saddle which could be used uncovered.

BRIDLE. Light cavalry model with slight regimental peculiarities.

PORTE-MANTEAU. On campaign the porte-manteau was supposed to contain two shirts, two cravats, two handkerchiefs, a pair of trousers or pantaloons, a waistcoat, the *bonnet de police*, the stable jacket, a spare pair of boots and *la trousse*.

Exactly how the Chasseurs fitted on all the bits and pieces they were meant to carry was something of a mystery even to Commandant Bucquoy. In the First World War it was noticed that French cavalry tended to overload their horses. It rather looks as if this was a time-honoured custom!

Armorial bearings of a Count of the Empire carried after March 1808

Uniforms of the Imperial Guard

On 18 May 1804 the Consular Guard took the title of Imperial Guard. The change of name made little real difference to the dress of the Chasseurs, who, as we have seen in the previous chapter, had already adopted the uniform which they were to wear throughout the period of the Empire. There was, however, some modification of badges.

COLBACK. The pattern of pompom was now changed for the last time – it was to be a semi-spherical tricolor pompom-cockade; the blue centre being embroidered with an eagle of orange cloth.

In 1809 Lefèbvre-Desnöuettes wanted to introduce a red plume, and Lejeune's painting of Somo-Sierra shows the chasseurs wearing it, but it did not survive the Spanish campaign of that year.

GIBERNE. A brass eagle replaced the horn.

EQUIPMENT. In 1806–7 black leather equipment of Prussian origin was issued.

SABRETACHE. The pattern with a red background worn under the consulate was replaced by one of green cloth with the Imperial arms. Several still exist. This pattern remained in use until 1815.

SCHABRAQUE. The eagle embroidered in orange cloth replaced the horns at the rear angles of the schabraque.

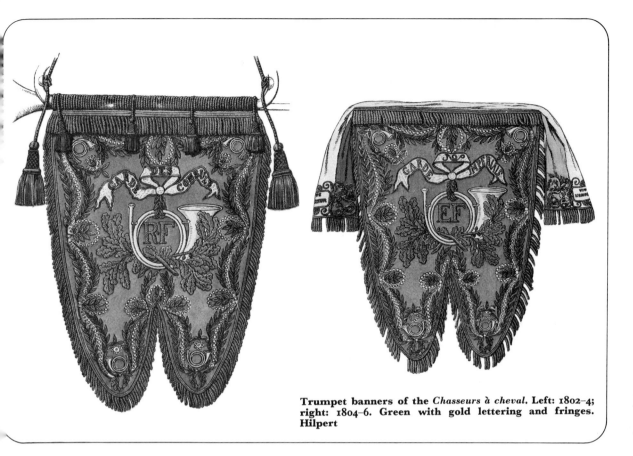

Trumpet banners of the *Chasseurs à cheval.* **Left: 1802–4; right: 1804–6. Green with gold lettering and fringes. Hilpert**

CULOTTE. Although there are a few plates which show chasseurs in red trousers, and although officers occasionally wore them, it is thought that they were never really a general issue to the Regiment. Although there are a number of plates by German artists which purport to show the uniform of the Chasseurs, these generally contain a number of errors and must therefore be regarded with suspicion. Bucquoy has put us on our guard against the plates of Kolbe and Weiland.

A document of 15 December 1812 lists the items issued to each chasseur on arrival. It was not a new regulation but a statement of things as they were at that time. Two minor points are worth noting: the stable jacket was decorated with two rows of buttons, and the old leather pantaloons had been replaced by ones trimmed with cloth and with orange borders.

CHABRAQUE of 1814. In 1814 the squadrons of the Young Guard had red schabraques. It is possible that they were also issued to the Old Guard. At the sale of the Castanie Collection in 1899, the schabraque which had belonged to a chasseur named Merme was sold. It was red, the front trimmed with leather, the seat of white sheepskin and was lined with leather and cloth. In 1814 Merme had been posted to the *éclaireurs* as an instructor. It is possible that this means he had gone to the Young Guard. A portrait of an officer which appeared in the same sale, and seemed to date from 1814, also showed a red schabraque. These clues rather make it look as if there was a general issue of red schabraques to the whole Corps between 1813 and 1814.

NCOS. There was little change in the turnout of NCOs under the Empire. The sabretache was the same as that of the Chasseurs except that it had gold ornamentation, and the eagles on their schabraques seem to have been made from metal thread instead of orange cloth.

CORPS ROYAL DES CHASSEURS DE FRANCE

The Restoration changed very little in the uniform of the Corps except for the emblems. The

A well-known painting by Gericault showing Lieutenant Dieudonné

eagles, of course, disappeared for the time being and were replaced by the escutcheon of France surmounted by the Royal Crown and surrounded by a wreath. The eagle also disappeared from the schabraque but nothing was put in its place. A white pompom, or possibly a white plume, replaced the green and red pompom formerly in use.

THE HUNDRED DAYS

The Imperial insignia was not slow to reappear when the Emperor returned in 1814. For the Waterloo Campaign, riding trousers resembling those in use under the Consulate were issued. The Regiment did not receive pelisses.

OFFICERS

For officers, as for men, the change from Consulate to Empire meant little except a change of badges. There are plenty of pictures of officers in full dress. Of these, perhaps the spirited portrait of Lieutenant Dieudonné by Gèricault is the best known. It was displayed in the Salon in 1812. Dieudonné was wounded on 7 December 1812 on the Vilna road and died next day. A number of other portraits survive, the subjects including Eugène, Lefèbvre-Desnöuettes, Zickel and others.

ARMAMENT

Under the Empire the officers carried a sabre with a hilt of gilded brass. The blade was often very ornamental and had a crowned eagle and the inscription 'Chasseurs à Cheval de la Garde Impériale'.

SABRETACHE. This was sometimes made of green velvet on the same general lines as that of the troopers but with all their orange ornaments being replaced with gold.

HARNESS. In full dress the officers had a schabraque of panther skin.

TRUMPETERS AND KETTLE-DRUMMERS

At the beginning of the Empire there was little change in the dress of the trumpeters, except for

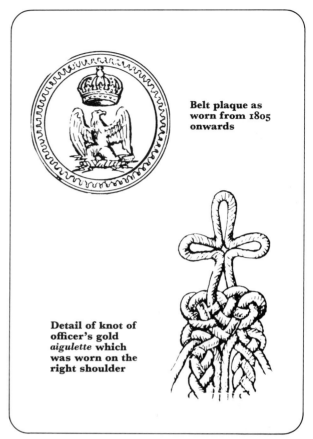

Belt plaque as worn from 1805 onwards

Detail of knot of officer's gold *aigulette* which was worn on the right shoulder

the usual Imperial insignia and, in general, the same uniform was worn throughout the Empire.

The kettle-drummer wore Mameluke costume. There are many versions of this uniform. For some time the kettle-drummer was Bruno Lemoine, whose portrait and sabretache are in the *Musée de l'Armée*. He wears a Hussar uniform. He became corporal trumpeter in 1805, though still appearing sometimes as kettle-drummer and was killed in 1808 in a combat at Torquemada. The Mameluke costume was worn between 1805 and 1806 and thereafter was superseded by the Hussar costume.

SAPEURS

Some of the Alsatian collections show a group of *sapeurs* with tremendous beards and crossed axes embroidered on their arms, but there is nothing to confirm that they ever existed in reality.

CAMPAIGN UNIFORM. In 1805 the Regiment wore the pelisse but it fought at Austerlitz in full dress. The cloak was often rolled up and worn bandolier fashion, *à la Mandrin*, as this was called; a reference to the celebrated French bandit of the early eighteenth century. In 1806 and 1807 the regiment wore the green *surtout* because the scarlet of the pelisse had been found to run and fade too much under the hard conditions of active service. In bad weather they put a cover over the colpack and wore a cape over their cloaks. 1808: General Lejeune's picture of the Battle of Somo-Sierra shows the uniform worn in Spain. 1809: the last five campaigns of the Empire were made in the dolman only. The leather trousers were left at the depot and so were the *surtouts*. The cloth trousers known as *hongroise* were worn. 1815: for the campaign in Belgium the turnout was simplified. Plumes were not worn and nor were cordons. The pantaloon or overall replaced the culotte. The only difference between the dress worn on the march and that for escort duty was that in the latter order the *flamme* of the colback was allowed to float freely.

We are not concerned here with the uniform of the Young Guard Regiment or of the Mamelukes. As far as the Old Guard Regiment is concerned,

Officer's pelisse trimmed with light grey fur. The eight chevrons on the sleeve distinguish it as that worn by a General of the Guard

and despite a mass of varied information, one receives the impression that the Regiment stuck as far as possible to its original and traditional uniform, making really very little change from its original appearance under the Consulate.

Guidons and Standards

'*Les étendards que la Garde à cheval à reçus hier à la parade, doivent être toujours pour elle le point de rassemblement contre les ennemis du Gouvernement. La plus gloire sera toujours un dévouement sans bornes à la personne du Premier Consul.*'

Regimental Orders, 23 January 1804

CONSULATE

Sous-Lieutenant Nicolas Le Gros who had won a carbine of honour was nominated Standard-bearer on 1 August 1801. We may assume, therefore, that from this period the squadron carried Standards. The Standard-bearer of the second squadron, nominated on 1 October, was Sous-Lieutenant Joseph Guibert, the holder of a sabre of honour. These Standards were carried at the religious ceremony for the promulgation of the Concordat and at the national holiday which marked the general peace after the Treaty of Amiens (1802). These Standards were in fact embroidered Guidons of crimson damask.

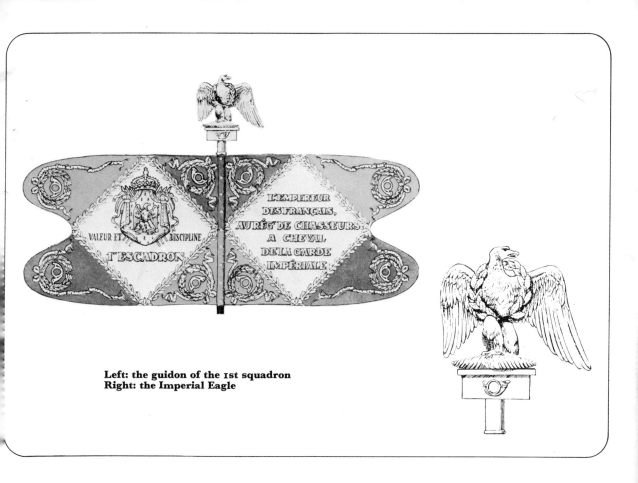

Left: the guidon of the 1st squadron
Right: the Imperial Eagle

In October 1802 the Standard-bearers were:

1st squadron – Joseph Guibert
2nd squadron – Antoine Peyrot
3rd squadron – Paul Pailhès
4th squadron – Robert Addet

From a letter of Beauharnais to the War Ministry we find that on 28 November 1802, the regimental regalia included 2 Standards with red backgrounds; 16 green trumpet banners, full dress; 17 green trumpet banners, undress; 1 pair of kettle-drums; 2 green kettle-drum banners like those for the trumpets. These were embroidered by Madame Challiot of 7, rue Boucherat, au Marais, who overcharged for them! The kettle-drums were made by le sieur Cagnor of No 36, rue du Petit Carreau.

The Proclamation of the Empire (18 May 1804), brought changes to the Colours as well as the uniforms of the regiment. The Imperial Eagle now appeared at the top of the poles.

From 1804 to 1812 the regiment carried 4 Tricolour Guidons. From 1813 to 1814 and during the Hundred Days, it had one Tricolour Standard (not a Guidon). After the reorganization of 15 April 1806, the regiment, in common with

Trumpet and banner. Full dress, 1804–5. Silver trumpet, green banner with gold trimmings and ornaments. After Hoffmann

33

**Chasseurs standing guard over the person of the Emperor
at the Battle of Smolensk, 17 August 1812**

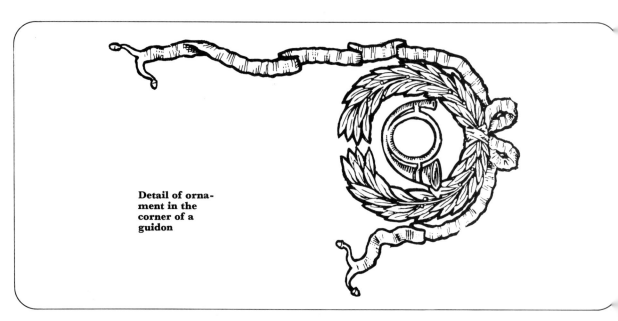

**Detail of orna-
ment in the
corner of a
guidon**

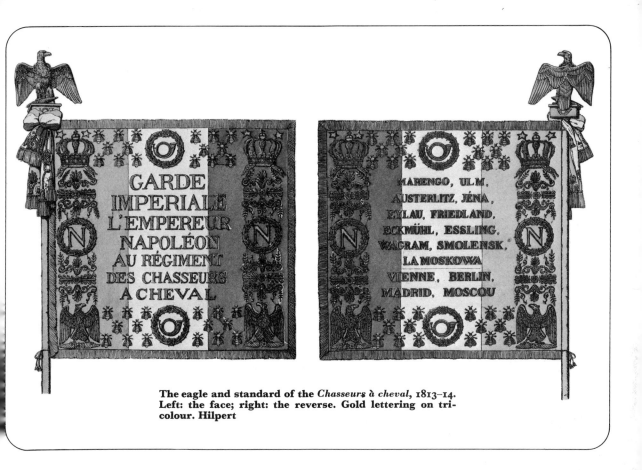

The eagle and standard of the *Chasseurs à cheval*, 1813–14. Left: the face; right: the reverse. Gold lettering on tricolour. Hilpert

others of the cavalry of the Guard, received new trumpet and kettle-drum banners completely different from the old ones. The new trumpet banners were square with gold fringes; were crimson instead of green and the Imperial escutcheon embroidered in gold appeared in the centre.

On 21 November 1807 when the Imperial Guard returned to Paris after the campaigns in Prussia and Poland, the Prefect of La Seine, one Frochot, presented on behalf of the city of Paris gold crowns which were to be attached to the Eagles of the regiment of the *Chasseurs à cheval* in commemoration of the victory of Austerlitz.

By decree of 1 July 1813, the Eagle of the 1st quadron became the regimental Standard and the Standard-bearers of the 2nd, 3rd and 4th quadrons were suppressed. The new Standard which was now attached to the Eagle bore the names of the victories at which the regiment had been present, from Marengo to La Moskowa (Borodino).

THE RESTORATION

With the Restoration of 1814, the Corps had of course a new Standard which was designed by le sieur Gastel of the dépôt de la Guerre. This Standard was probably received when the regiment was in garrison at Saumur in December 1814. It was not destined to be carried in action.

THE HUNDRED DAYS

The Emperor distributed Eagles on the Champ de Mai on 1 June 1815, the Chasseurs receiving a Standard similar to the one carried in 1813. Whether or not battle honours for the campaigns of 1813 and 1814 were added, we cannot tell.

When the Imperial Army was disbanded after Waterloo, the Guard was ordered to hand in its Eagles to the artillery headquarters at Bourges. On 31 August 1815 the regiment delivered one Eagle and one Standard with the usual attachments; these were destroyed on the orders of the Ministry on 22 October.

Napoleon in his study, from a painting by Delaroche. He is wearing the undress uniform of a colonel of the chasseurs

YOUNG GUARD

The second regiment of *Les Chasseurs à cheval de la Garde Impériale*, created by Imperial decree on 26 May 1815, received a Standard from the Emperor on 1 June. It was similar to that of other cavalry regiments. This was also destroyed on 22 October.

MAMELUKES

Legend would make one think that the Mamelukes carried a sort of Oriental Standard with a horse's tail floating from it but, in fact, they seem to have carried Guidons and Standards much like any other cavalry regiment.

The decree of 25 December 1811, which laid down that no cavalry corps of less than 600 men should have an Eagle, was not applied to the Mamelukes.

The names of two of the Standard-bearers have been preserved; they were: Sous-Lieutenant Pierre Mèrat, 18 December 1805 and Jean-François Fonnade, 6 December 1811 to 5 August 1814.

SELECT BIBLIOGRAPHY

Le Captaine E.-L. Bucquoy, O. Hollander and P. Benigni: *Les Chasseurs à cheval de la Garde Impériale* (1800–15).

D. G. Chandler: *The Campaigns of Napoleon* (New York, 1966).

Commandant H. Lachouque and Anne Browne: *The Anatomy of Glory* (London and New York, 1961).

A. Martinien: *Tableaux par Corps et par Batailles des Officiers Tués et Blessés pendant les Guerres de l'Empire* (Paris, n.d.).

Charles Parquin: *Military Memoirs*, translated and edited by B. T. Jones (London, 1969).

Jean-Claude Quennevat: *Les Vrais Soldats de Napoleon* (Paris and Brussels, 1968).

Lucien Rousselot: *Armée Française*, Planches Nos. 69, 70 and 94.

Albert Schuermans: *Itinéraire Générale de Napoleon Ier* (Paris, 1911).

Georges Six: *Dictionnaire Biographique des Généraux et Amiraux de la Révolution et de l'Empire (1792–1814)*. (Paris, 1934.)

NOTES

1. General Baron Jean-Baptiste-Juvenal Corbineau (1776–1848).

2. I regret to observe that a modern Michelin Guide makes no mention of this hotel!

3. Edward-Jean-Baptiste comte Milhaud (1766–1833).

4. Horace-François-Bastien, comte Sébastiani de la Porta (1772–1851), Marshal of France, 1840.

5. The author has dragged this in because his own regiment, later the 16th Foot, defeated the French cavalry single handed!

6. Or *gilet d'écurie*.

7. *Tricot*.

APPENDIX A

Numbers of Officers killed and wounded. 1805–15

1805		K	DW	W	Total
22 Oct.	Affair near Ulm	–	–	1	1
20 Nov.	On escort duty with Marshal Bessières	–	–	1	1
2 Dec.	Battle of Austerlitz	2	–	17	19
1806					
25 Dec.	Affair of Lopaczyn	–	–	1	1
1807					
8 Feb.	Battle of Eylau	1	4	12	17
10 June	Battle of Heilsberg	–	–	1	1
14 June	Battle of Friedland	–	–	1	1
1808					
2 May	Insurrection in Madrid	–	–	8	8
29 Dec.	Combat of Benavente	1	–	5	6
1809					
4 July	Crossing the Danube	–	–	1	1
6 July	Battle of Wagram	4	–	10	14
1810					
18 June	Escorting prisoners in Spain	–	–	1	1
1811					
2 May	Combat of Carascal, Spain	–	–	1	1
1812					
10 Feb.	On a mobile column in Spain	–	1	–	1
23 April	Combat of Robrez, Spain	–	–	1	1
14 Oct.	At the outposts before Moscow	–	–	1	1
15 Oct.	Combat on the Kalouga road	–	–	1	1
24 Oct.	Battle of Malojaroslawetz	–	–	1	1
25 Oct.	Combat near Malojaroslawetz	–	–	1	1
17 Nov.	Battle of Krasnoë	–	1	–	1
21 Nov.	Combat on the Borisow road	–	–	1	1
7 Dec.	On the Vilna road	–	1	–	1
1813					
2 May	Battle of Lutzen	–	–	1	1
22 May	Combat of Reichenbach	–	–	2	2
26-7 Aug.	Battle of Dresden	–	–	3	3
26 Sept.	Affair before Altenbourg	–	–	1	1

		K	DW	W	Total
27 Sept.	Combat before Altenbourg	–	–	1	1
14 Oct.	Combat near Magdebourg	–	–	1	1
18 Oct.	Battle of Leipzig	1	–	6	7
23 Oct.	Combat of Weimar	1	–	3	4
27 Oct.	Affair of Wach	–	–	1	1
29–30 Oct.	Battle of Hanau	–	–	3	3
27 Dec.	Combat before Breda	–	–	1	1
31 Dec.	On reconnaissance near Breda	–	–	1	1
1814					
29 Jan.	Battle of Brienne	–	–	1	1
11 Feb.	Battle of Montmirail	–	–	1	1
12 Feb.	Combat of Château-Thierry	1	–	1	2
18 Feb.	Battle of Montereau	–	–	1	1
1 Mar.	Affair of Lisy	–	–	1	1
4 Mar.	Combat before Soissons	–	–	1	1
7 Mar.	Battle of Craonne	1	–	4	5
11 Mar.	Combat before Soissons	–	–	1	1
11 Mar.	Combat near Laon	–	–	1	1
17 Mar.	Combat of Braine	–	–	1	1
30 Mar.	Battle of Paris	–	–	1	1
31 Mar.	Combat of Courtrai	–	–	4	4
1815					
18 June	Battle of Waterloo	5	1	14	20

COMPANY OF MAMELUKES (SQUADRON IN 1813)

1805		K	DW	W	Total
2 Dec.	Battle of Austerlitz	–	–	3	3
1806					
25 Dec.	Affair of Lopaczyn	–	–	1	1
26 Dec.	Combat of Golymin	–	–	1	1
1807					
8 Feb.	Battle of Eylau	–	–	3	3
1808					
2 May	Insurrection in Madrid	–	–	5	5
4 Aug.	Attack on Saragossa	–	–	1	1
29 Dec.	Combat of Benavente	1	–	1	2
1813					
28 Sept.	Combat of Altenbourg	–	–	2	2
23 Oct.	Combat of Weimar	–	–	1	1
30 Oct.	Battle of Hanau	–	–	1	1

APPENDIX B

Senior Officer casualties

CHASSEURS À CHEVAL

Colonel

Morland	K	Battle of Austerlitz	2 Dec. 1805

Chef d'Éscadrons

Nicolas-Marin Thiry (1769–1827)	SW	Battle of Austerlitz	2 Dec. 1805
Frédéric-Auguste Beurmann (1777–1815)	W	Battle of Austerlitz	2 Dec. 1805
Charpentier	W	Battle of Austerlitz	2 Dec. 1805
Nicolas-Marin Thiry	W	Battle of Eylau	8 Feb. 1807
Pierre Daumesnil (1777–1832)	W	Insurrection in Madrid	2 May 1808

Gen. de Brigade

Lefèbvre-Desnöuettes (1773–1822)	W & PW	Combat of Benavente	29 Dec. 1808

Chef d'Éscadrons

Pierre Daumesnil	W	Battle of Eckmühl	22 May 1809
Francq	W	Battle of Wagram	6 July 1809

Major

Corbineau	SW	Battle of Wagram	6 July 1809
Pierre Daumesnil	SW	Battle of Wagram	6 July 1809

Chef d'Éscadrons

Kirmann	W	Combat near Malojaroslavetz	25 Oct. 1812
Lafitte	W	Battle of Leipzig	18 Oct. 1813
Kirmann	W	Battle of Leipzig	18 Oct. 1813
Janot	W	Combat of Weimar	23 Oct. 1813
Lemercier	W	Combat of Weimar	23 Oct. 1813
Joannès	W	Battle of Hanau	30 Oct. 1813
Lemercier	W	Affair of Lisy	1 Mar. 1814
Blanquefort	W	Battle of Waterloo	18 June 1815
Lafitte	W	Battle of Waterloo	18 June 1815

MAMELUKES

Chef d'Éscadrons

Antoine-Charles-Bernard Delaitre (1776–1838)	W	Affair of Lopaczyn	25 Dec. 1806

K—Killed, DW—Died of wounds, SW—Severely wounded, W—Wounded, PW—Prisoner of war

The Plates

A *Lieutenant, Standard Bearer, Full Dress 1808*
He wears the Hussar uniform and the standard is a guidon. *Source*, plate by P. Benigni in Captain E.-L. Bucquoy's publication *Les Uniformes du 1ᵉʳ Empire*.

B *Trumpeter, Full Dress 1803*
His sabretache is of the normal type in use under the Consulate, crimson, trimmed with gold lace. The porte-manteau is blue, probably because it was used in all weathers, and had it been crimson like the full-dress sabretache would have faded in no time, for crimson is not a durable colour.

C *Chasseur 1805–14*
Full Dress as worn on service, when on escort duty with the Emperor.

D1 *Chasseur, Full Dress, 1800*
From Isabey's painting *La Revue de decadi*.

D2 *Chef de Brigade Eugène de Beauharnais, 1800*
From a painting by Carle Vernet.

D3 *Officer, Full Dress Consulate*
After Hoffmann.

E1 *Chasseur, 1803–4*
He is wearing his pelisse as a jacket. This was the uniform worn on Sundays in the winter. *Source*, the Regimental Order Book.

E2 *Officer, 1804*
The red breeches were probably never 'regulation' but a *tenue de fantaisie*. *Source*, the Regimental Order Book.

E3 *Chasseur, 1803–4*
The uniform worn on week-days in winter. *Source*, the Regimental Order Book.

F1 *Chasseur, Battle of Austerlitz, 1805*
The pelisse is worn as a jacket, and the cloak worn bandolier fashion and gives some protection against sword cuts.

F2 *Chasseur, campaign of 1806*
Uniform worn by pickets when on duty on foot guarding the Emperor's person.

F3 *Chasseur, campaigns of 1806 and 1807*
Uniform worn on mounted escort duty in foul weather.

G1 *Officer, 1812–14*
On the march. After Horace Vernet.

G2 *Officer, 1808*
The uniform worn at Somosierra. After Marbot.

G3 *Chasseur, 1808*
Uniform worn on the march in Spain. After General Baron Lejeune.

H1 *Chef de musique, 1810*
The bandmaster was evidently a Senior NCO.

H2 *Kettle-drummer, 1805*
After Hoffmann.

H3 *Trumpeter, 1801*